THE MORNING DEW

56 DAYS OF INSPIRATIONS TO SOOTHE THE DOUBT AND
CALM THE FEAR

BY
DEBORAH BASS-HARPER

Printed in the United States of America

Copyright © 2019 Deborah Harper

First Printing, 2019

ISBN: 9781701372450

ORDERING INFORMATION:

Quantity Sales: Special discounts are available on quantity purchases by corporations, associations, and others via

deborah.pastor14@gmail.com

**Book Cover Design: Bobby Barnhill
Editing : LakeView Publishing
Publishing: LakeView Publishing**

Dedication

I dedicate to all God's children who are seeking the kingdom of God and His righteousness. To those who are not, I pray this daily inspirational devotional is a blessing to you.

I dedicate this book to those who desire to press toward the mark of the high calling of God in Christ Jesus.

I dedicate this book to those who desire to destroy the curses spoken over their life before birth.

I dedicate this book to those who are with one accord. The Holy Spirit is your guide, and you are waiting for the manifestations of the things God has spoken to you.

I dedicate this book to all the faithful ones waiting for a move of God. Be encouraged your hope is not in vain!

"Sometimes situations can cause you to lose focus of the things God has spoken to you, but it's our responsibility to remain focused on God."

~ DEBORAH

CHAPTER INDEX

INTRODUCTION

THE MORNING DEW

56 DAYS OF INSPIRATIONS TO SOOTHETHE DOUBT AND CALM THE FEAR

BY
DEBORAH BASS-HARPER

INTRODUCTION

Good morning people of God!

By way of introduction, God said to tell My people, "When God works, no matter how long it takes, it will be worth the wait."

This book is designed to catapult you into your next level with the Lord!

"There is a season (a time appointed) for everything and a time for every delight and event or purpose under heaven."

~ Ecclesiastes 3:1 (amp)

"A time to search and a time to give up as lost; a time to keep and a time to throw away."

~ Ecclesiastes 3:6 (amp)

It is the plan of God, how the Holy Spirit wants to speak through His people. HE desires to conduit His power through us, using us as a vessel, a house of prayer, giving us words of exhortation, words of inspiration to motivate one another in such a time as this. He desires to empower us to keep one another lifted in the name of Jesus. God knows His people are in a season of waiting. They are waiting for a movement of God like the people at the Bethesda pool waited for healing. What you are about to read is a book made up of fifty-six daily inspirational messages from God to you. The writings, along with scriptures from the Word of God, to place in your heart and meditate on, will strengthen and empower you while you wait.

By using these two resources together, you will find that it will pave a clear path to your pool of healing. Scripture always charges your atmosphere to a level where it can become conducive for God's miracles to manifest in our life.

This book will be a blessing that will help you get to your next.

Be blessed!

~ Deborah

DAY 1

THE BEGINNING: DON'T MESS WITH GOD'S PLAN

What a marvelous morning we have been given, and The Father created it.

God has a plan for everyone's life. The question is, what makes you so unique that God would give you the divine plan He has for your life?

The answer is nothing. You are no better than the next person. It's your praise and worship and obedience amid your trials and tribulations that catapult you closer in the presence of God — allowing God to use your temple as a place of habitation so you can be used by God to do His will.

Let us remain humble towards the things of God and keeping yourself lifted by meditating on the word of God. He is using you. There is a breach in the spirit, and your voice is needed in such a time as this. Now give

God all the praise because he is worthy. God said it, and it is so.

"And Jacob went out from Beersheba, and went toward Haran. And he lighted upon a certain place, and tarried there all night, because the sun was set; and he took of the stones of that place, and put them for his pillows, and lay down in that place to sleep. And he dreamed, and behold a ladder set up on the earth, and the top of it reached to heaven: and behold the angels of God ascending and descending on it. And, behold, the Lord stood above it, and said, I am the Lord God of Abraham thy father, and the God of Isaac: the land whereon thou liest, to thee will I give it, and to thy seed; And thy seed shall be as the dust of the earth, and thou shalt spread abroad to the west, and to the east, and to the north, and to the south: and in thee and in thy seed shall all the families of the earth be blessed. And, behold, I am with thee, and will keep thee in all places whither thou goest, and will bring thee again into this land; for I will not leave thee, until I have done that which I have spoken to thee of. And Jacob awaked out of his sleep, and he said, Surely the Lord is in this place; and I knew it not. And he was afraid, and said, How dreadful is this place! This is none other but the house of God, and this is the gate of heaven.

~ Genesis 28:10-17 (KJV)

" O give thanks unto the Lord, for he is good: for his mercy endureth for ever. Let the redeemed of the Lord say so, whom he hath redeemed from the hand of the enemy;"

~ Psalm 107: 1-2 (KJV)

DAY 2

A FLIPPED SCRIPT: YES, IT'S A GOOD THING

Good morning people of God!

After several days of listening to the Holy Spirit and writing as He gives me the unction, I felt a turn. He reminded me of a vision I had seen many years ago. I heard the Holy Spirit say, "Return to that place where I baptized you with the Holy Ghost, the place where you began speaking with many tongues as the Holy Ghost gave you the utterance."

Sometimes situations can cause you to lose focus on the things God has spoken to you, but it's our responsibility to remain focused on God.

After many days of writing, here I am, with a new beginning. I am viewing life differently, and while the vision is old, it's new. This life is the beginning of a new beginning.

Now you see how God can do whatever He wants? Whenever He wants, and however, He wants because He is God.

Your job is to stay tuned, stay focused, keep the faith, and be ready to move when the Spirit says move.

I COME TO MAKE YOU RUN!

"And the LORD answered me, and said, write the vision, and make it plain upon tables, that he may run that readeth it. For the vision is yet for an appointed time, but at the end it shall speak, and not lie: though it tarry, wait for it; because it will surely come, it will not tarry."

~ Habakkuk 2:2-3 (KJV)

"But they that wait upon the Lord shall renew their strength; they shall mount up with wings as eagles; they shall run, and not be weary; and they shall walk, and not faint."

~ Isaiah 40:31 (KJV)

DAY 3

KEEP THE FAITH

Good morning!

You may be experiencing spiritual drought in your life, maybe financial decline, or just so much on your mind until it's a burden too heavy for you to bear. I want to encourage you today:

Continue to move forward, and distractions will come, the purpose is to derail you from purpose, to see and understand your purpose; you must keep your eyes on God.

You must press toward the mark for the prize of the high calling of God in Christ Jesus, put no confidence in the flesh, and place all your trust in God. This the Lord's doings and it is marvellous workmanship of God.

God woke me up this morning with this powerful word in my heart to publish, God said, tell my people to move forward toward the things of God. Be obedient and keep pressing forward. I encourage you to keep the faith. You will surely connect with the promises God made you. Don't lose hope.

SHE HEARD, SHE PRESSED, AND GOD BLESSED

"So then faith cometh by hearing, and hearing by the word of God."

~ **Romans 10:17-21 (KJV)**

"And without faith it is impossible to please him, for whoever would draw near to God must believe that he exists and that he rewards those who seek him."

~ **Hebrews 11:6 (ESV)**

"Then a woman who had suffered from a haemorrhage for twelve years came up behind Him and touched the [tassel] fringe of His outer robe; for she had been saying to herself, "If I only touch His outer robe, I will be healed." But Jesus turning and seeing her said, "Take courage, daughter; your [personal trust and confident] faith [in Me] has made you well." And at once the woman was [completely] healed."

~ **Matthew 9:20-22 (AMP)**

DAY 4

YOU'RE DELIVERED! NOW KEEP THE FAITH

Good morning!

I want to give you some encouragement to remember. When God has delivered you, there's no going backward. You have been made free. You must continue to move forward to see the promises of God.

Do not allow the rabble to re-enter your life with negative talk; it only causes confusion, the warfare of the mind.

You know what God has charged you to do, so you must do it. It's not about you. It has always been and will always be about Christ and the power of His resurrection.

Separate yourself from negativity, focus on positivity, and allow God to form you into His great workmanship. God has need of you.

THE LORD WANTS TO USE YOU FOR HIS SERVICE

"After Jesus had said this, he went on ahead, going up to Jerusalem. As he approached Bethphage and Bethany at the hill called the Mount of Olives, he sent two of his disciples, saying to them, Go to the village ahead of you, and as you enter it, you will find a colt tied there, which no one has ever ridden. Untie it and bring it here. If anyone asks you, 'Why are you untying it?' say, 'The Lord needs it.'" Those who were sent ahead went and found it just as he had told them. As they were untying the colt, its owners asked them, "Why are you untying the colt?" They replied, "The Lord needs it." They brought it to Jesus, threw their cloaks on the colt and put Jesus on it."

~ Luke 19:28-35 (NIV)

DAY 5

DON'T WORRY GOD HAS BLESSED YOU: IT HAPPENED ON THE THIRD DAY.

Good morning!

Praise God for another spiritual level. Jesus rose on the third day, and so should we, as we seek a closer walk with God. An enlarged territory, free from things that once irritated you or whatever issue that was blocking you from your spiritual freedom.

Just thank God for the rain, the abundance of blessings flowing, and the instructions He has given you to maintain your freedom. This is a daily walk with God.

There is no need to worry about anything. Whatever you need, the Lord has it. He came through last night like a mighty rushing wind, answering prayers and delivering His people from bondage.

He has answered prayers you've been praying for a long time. It's done! The transition has taken place, and there's nothing anyone can do about it. Give God your best praise, for He has done great and mighty things.

USE WHAT GOD HAS PLACED IN YOUR HANDS

"Then Moses stretched out his hand over the sea, and all that night the Lord drove the sea back with a strong east wind and turned it into dry land. The waters were divided, and the Israelites went through the sea on dry ground, with a wall of water on their right and on their left."

~ Exodus 14:21-22 (NIV)

"The King is mighty, he loves justice--you have established equity; in Jacob you have done what is just and right. Exalt the Lord our God and worship at his footstool; he is holy."

~ Psalms 99:4, 5 (NIV)

DAY 6

CHECK YOURSELF

Good morning people of God!

What a powerful word God has given me to share
with His people around the world.

God is a Spirit, and His worshipers must worship Him
in the spirit and truth. But how can you give God
clean praise, clean worship, or sacrifice without a
pure heart? How can we make His Word a lamp unto
every step we take if we don't first allow the Holy
Spirit to give us a divine deep cleansing from
heaven?

There's nothing wrong with asking for God to help
you to worship Him in spirit and truth.

We aren't perfect people, although we strive for perfection. You must want to be cleansed, healed, and delivered by God, so our worship will be a pleasing aroma in the nostrils of God.

NOW RUN AND TELL THAT

"At this, Jesus said, "go, call your husband and come back." The woman answered, "I do not have a husband." Jesus said to her, "you have correctly said 'i do not have a husband. For you have had five husbands, and the man you are now living with is not your husband. You have said this truthfully." The woman said to him, "Sir, I see that you are a prophet."

~ John 4:16-19 amplified

"Then the woman left her water jar, and went into the city and began telling the people, come, see a man who told me all things that I have done! Can this be the Christ (messiah, the anointed)?" So the people left the city and were coming to him."

~ John 4:28-30 (amp)

DAY 7

IT'S IN THE TASTE

Good morning people of God!

Do you remember ever popping the cork on a bottle of wine after the aging process? This reaction is how our worship should be, a sweet-smelling fruity aroma, from our spirit into the nostrils of God.

You want God to tell you how intrigued He is with your worship. A fruity sweet smell lets us know we have truly connected with the fruits of the Spirit. It's your pure, aged, clean worship that will open the doors to your destiny.

God has placed the fruits in your hands, all the fruit that you can carry from the land that flows with milk and honey.

God has blessed the fruits of your labor.

BE FRUITFUL

"But the fruit of the Spirit [the result of His presence within us] is love [unselfish concern for others], joy, [inner] peace, patience [not the ability to wait, but how we act while waiting], kindness, goodness, faithfulness, gentleness, self-control. Against such things there is no law."

~ Galatians 5:22,23 (AMP)

"For you shall eat the fruit of [the labour of] your hands, You will be happy and blessed and it will be well with you."

~ Psalms 128:2 (AMP)

DAY 8

IT'S IN THE PRESS

Good morning!

What are you expecting from God? I'm reminded of the woman with an issue of blood.

Are you currently dealing with severe issues with your health or maybe family members have been stricken with an illness?

God says to tell His people, He hears your prayers, and He knows you are pressing through by meditating, trusting, and believing the scriptures of the Bible.

Let me encourage you this morning: your "suddenly" is in the pressing. Your breakthrough is in the pressing. The anointing will flow because of the pressing. You will receive strength in the pressing. It is alright to get tired, but you must keep pressing.

Just as God opened the door of healing for the woman with the issue of blood, He will do the same for you. Keep pressing your way into your suddenly.

And suddenly, you will hear the Holy Spirit say, "Woman, thy faith hath made you whole."

YOUR SUDDENLY IS HERE

"I will extol and praise You, O Lord, for You have lifted me up, And have not let my enemies rejoice over me. O Lord my God, I cried to You for help, and You have healed me. O Lord, You have brought my life up from Sheol (the nether world, the place of the dead); You have kept me alive, so that I would not go down to the pit (grave). Sing to the Lord, O you His godly ones, And give thanks at the mention of His holy name. For His anger is but for a moment His favor is for a lifetime. Weeping may endure for a night, but a shout of joy comes in the morning."

~ Psalms 30:1-5 (AMP)

"But Jesus turning and seeing her said, "Take courage, daughter; your [personal trust and confident] faith [in Me has made you well." And at once the woman was [completely] healed."

~ Matthew 9:22 (AMP)

DAY 9

RESSURECTION MANIFESTATIONS

Good morning!

Everything God created is good.

Even when life throws you sour, rotten fruit such as lemons, rotten apples that appear to be dead, or how about those crab-apples that will make you frown and smack your lips! Sometimes we are tempted even to say; this isn't good at all. Sometimes you will say a circumstance is not of God, or a season of life will make you feel like throwing it down.

Everything God created is good. We are born in sin and shaped in iniquity.

God plans to lead you to the potter's wheel to correct the errors you made during life's journey.

There is goodness in the midst of that very thing that brought havoc in your life. A situation is not always how it appears. Often, our biggest pains is a blessing in disguise. It was handed to you because God has prepared you to speak life in a bad situation. He created you to speak the words that have already been spoken. God will hear His word and certainly bless His word according to His will. You first must believe and see it happening in the spiritual realm

FROM THE HANDS THAT CREATED YOU

"So God created man in his own image, in the image of God created he him; male and female created he them."

~ Genesis 1:27(KJV)

"The word which came to Jeremiah from the LORD, saying, Arise, and go down to the potter's house, and there I will cause thee to hear my words. Then I went down to the potter's house, and, behold, he wrought a work on the wheels. And the vessel that he made of clay was marred in the hand of the potter: so he made it again another vessel, as seemed good to the potter to make it. Then the word of the LORD came to me, saying, O house of Israel, cannot I do with you as this potter? saith the LORD. Behold, as the clay is in the potter's hand, so are ye in mine hand, O house of Israel."

~ Jeremiah 18:1-6 (KJV)

DAY 10

SISTERS, HELP YOUR SISTERS

Good morning!

Ladies, there is a word this morning that God has ordained me to release to His women.

There is nothing wrong with you lifting one another in Jesus name. When you see one down, when you see one lacking knowledge, or when you see one in need of help, don't walk past your sister in need.

Don't look at them or with your nose in the air as if they don't even exist. God will bring that day back into remembrance because He loves you too much to let that slide. He will let you see faults.

It's good to remain humble and treat people like you want to be treated in the name of Christ Jesus.

So, do not pass your sister by when she is in need. After all the gift doesn't belong to you, it belongs to God. God will get the glory from all gifts that He has blessed you with. To God, be the glory!

SHOW KINDNESS!

"But the fruit of the Spirit is love, joy, peace, forbearance, kindness, goodness, faithfulness, gentleness and self-control. Against such things there is no law."

~ Galatians 5:22,23 (KJV)

"Give her of the fruit of her hands; and let her own works praise her in the gates."

~ Proverbs 31:31(KJV)

"And Ruth the Moabite said to Naomi, "Let me go to the fields and pick up the leftover grain behind anyone in whose eyes I find favor." Naomi said to her, "Go ahead, my daughter."

~ Ruth 2:2 (NIV)

"She carried it back to town, and her mother-in-law saw how much she had gathered. Ruth also brought out and gave her what she had left over after she had eaten enough."

~ Ruth 2:18 (NIV)

DAY 11

BELIEVE

Good morning!

I often hear people say, and while it's okay to get tired, don't ever give up on that vision God has spoken into your spirit, I want you to know it shall manifest soon. Believe what God has spoken to you.
The bible teaches us in the 5th chapter of Luke's gospel, verses 1-7, how the two men of God stepped away from their boat, to clean their nets. Sometimes in life, we become weary in our well-doing, simply because we grow tired of going around in circles, doing the same thing over again and never see anything new in our life.

Allow me to encourage you. There is an appointed time for things of God to manifest.

Be encouraged and wait on Jesus to enter in and give you divine launching instructions.

YOU BETTER BELIEVE WHAT GOD IS TELLING YOU!

"And he entered into one of the ships, which was Simon's, and prayed him that he would thrust out a little from the land. And he sat down and taught the people out of the ship. Now when he had left speaking, he said unto Simon, Launch out into the deep, and let down your nets for a draught. And Simon answering said unto him, Master, we have toiled all the night, and have taken nothing: nevertheless at thy word I will let down the net. And when they had this done, they in closed a great multitude of fishes: and their net brake. And they beckoned unto their partners, which were in the other ship, that they should come and help them. And they came, and filled both the ships, so that they began to sink. When Simon Peter saw it, he fell down at Jesus' knees, saying, depart from me; for I am a sinful man, O Lord. For he was astonished, and all that were with him, at the draught of the fishes which they had taken:"

$\sim$ **Luke 5:3-9(KJV)**

"And let us not be weary in well doing: for in due season we shall reap, if we faint not."

~ **Galatians 6:9 (KJV)**

DAY 12

CHECK YOUR FAITH LEVEL

Good morning!

Faith is the key that unlocks doors, without faith you cannot please God.

The door that is now open, always keep in mind, it's all about pleasing Abba Father, the true and living God.

F- Faith in action, now faith is confidence in what we hope for and assurance about what we do not see.

A- Ask, and it shall be given, seek, and he shall find, knock and the door shall open. Keep pulling on God and don't stop; He smells a sweet aroma coming from you. "Lord, do it for me!"

I-invite the Holy Spirit in, to rest, rule and abide right there inside your heart and where ever the Holy Spirit guides you.

T- Tell it to all the nations, (triumph)! God has given you victory.

H- Hold on to what you have so that no one will take your crown. Jesus is coming soon. HAVE FAITH IN WHAT WILL BE.

YOUR FAITH MOVES GOD

"Now faith is the substance of things hoped for, the evidence of things not seen. For by it the elders obtained a good report. Through faith we understand that the worlds were framed by the word of God, so that things which are seen were not made of things which do appear."

~ **Hebrews 11:1-3(KJV)**

"Women received their dead raised to life again: and others were tortured, not accepting deliverance; that they might obtain a better resurrection:"

~ **Proverbs 11:35(KJV)**

"And it came to pass after these things, that the son of the woman, the mistress of the house, fell sick; and his sickness was so sore, that there was no breath left in him. And she said unto Elijah, What have I to do with thee, O thou man of God? art thou come unto me to call my sin to remembrance, and to slay my son?

And he said unto her, Give me thy son. And he took him out of her bosom, and carried him up into a loft, where he abode, and laid him upon his own bed. And he cried unto the Lord, and said, O Lord my God, hast thou also brought evil upon the widow with whom I sojourn, by slaying her son? And he stretched himself upon the child three times, and cried unto the Lord, and said, O Lord my God, I pray thee, let this child's soul come into him again. And the Lord heard the voice of Elijah; and the soul of the child came into him again, and he revived. And Elijah took the child, and brought him down out of the chamber into the house, and delivered him unto his mother: and Elijah said, See, thy son liveth. And the woman said to Elijah, Now by this I know that thou art a man of God, and that the word of the Lord in thy mouth is truth."

~ 1 Kings 17:17-24 (KJV)

"Just as God opened the door of healing for the woman with the issue of blood, He will do the same for you."

~ DEBORAH

DAY 13

THE GLORY OF GOD

Good morning!

I heard the Holy Spirit say, "Increase." He then said, "The glory of God brings an increase in your life today!" He said, "Go in the kitchen." I went in the kitchen, and there I heard him say, "Look out the window." As I was opening the blinds, I saw two squirrels gathering food, and then there came another one, which made three squirrels now sitting in an old flower bed of mine that needs a little TLC. The squirrels got what they needed and left. This flower bed can be restored to its beauty even though the weeds and other stuff has made it ugly. As I went back to my desk, the Holy Spirit gave me the revelation to what my eyes had seen.

He said, "I never overlook people who seek my face. I will always help those who seek my face."

The Holy Spirit said, "Sometimes people can create "monsters" in their own life. Deadly monsters that will try to kill your spirit, like the weeds attempted to kill the beauty of the flower bed.

It happens, but you must remember there is a divine word that will kill any monsters we can create.

God always has a solution to every problem in your life. Even the Goliaths that desire to battle against you. (It's not your battle it's the Lord's) Give it to God, and allow Him to give you His instructions on how to kill the monsters that try to block you from destiny.

SOW AND YOU WILL GROW

"Now the Lord is that Spirit: and where the Spirit of the Lord is, there is liberty."

~ 2 Corinthians 3:17(KJV)

"While the earth remaineth, seedtime and harvest, and cold and heat, and summer and winter, and day and night shall not cease."

~ Genesis 8:22 (KJV)

"Blessed are those who wash their robes, that they may have the right to the tree of life and may go through the gates into the city."

~ Genesis 8:22 (KJV)

DAY 14

THE VISION

Good morning!

You often hear people say, "Don't tell anybody the vision God has given you. Even though it's hot off the press, meaning a Rhema word, straight from heaven, be quiet and don't say a word." You know that right now today, a word is burning in somebody's belly.

The Bible tells us the angel of the Lord came to Mary and told her, "You are blessed and highly favoured in the Lord. The Lord is with you!" He then said she would be impregnated with a baby, and His name will be called Jesus.

Mary found this troubling; first, she had to see what manner of man was this that was speaking to her in such a way. The Bible tells us that Mary pondered this divine encounter in her heart. I wasn't there, but I'm sure she was amazed.

That's how it is when the Holy Spirit delivers His messages and reveals who we are in His eyes and how He will use us in the kingdom building and reveals purpose to us. Amazing! God is still using His people to full-fill His purpose and his plans.

I also believe God will place people in your life in due season that will believe in your vision, and who will pray for you and be with you supporting the things of God. (Kingdom building). They will assist you in birthing your visions out. Just be still and know that I am with you.

DIVINE ADVANCEMENT

"And ye shall serve the Lord your God, and he shall bless thy bread, and thy water; and I will take sickness away from the midst of thee There shall nothing cast their young, nor be barren, in thy land: the number of thy days I will fulfil."

~ Exodus 23:25, 26 (KJV)

"For with God nothing shall be impossible."

~ Luke 1:37(KJV)

Be still, and know that I am God: I will be exalted among the heathen, I will be exalted in the earth. The LORD of hosts is with us; the God of Jacob is our refuge. Selah.

~ Psalms 46:10 - 11 (KJV)

DAY 15

THE COVENANT

Good morning!

After the rain and the flood, God made a covenant with Noah and sealed it with a rainbow. God promised that he would never again destroy the earth with floods.

Sometimes in life, even on your job, there's chaos like you never seen before. It comes to a point when you have to let go and let God. Letting go will bring you into one accord with the Spirit of the living God.

I'm thinking about how God felt back in Noah's day when He saw people doing whatever they wanted to do on earth. He found Noah to be righteous, and He chose Noah to build a masterpiece for Him. Noah followed specific instructions and accomplished the divine assignment. But others were doing whatever they wanted to do.

Some people also get tired of such, and the desire is to see something, a new thing, the promises God has made you, the desire to see God open new doors in the natural, the desire to see supernatural manifestation take place, and to see a change in people lives.

Today, is that new day, that new season, and it's taking place right now! Former things have passed away, the things that you once saw are no longer there. Today, God has done a new thing, and He has made life beautiful again according to His holy and divine will.

Let's praise and worship Abba Father for the great and marvellous things He has done.

A NEW MERCY!

And I saw a new heaven and a new earth: for the first heaven and the first earth were passed away; and there was no more sea. And I John saw the holy city, new Jerusalem, coming down from God out of heaven, prepared as a bride adorned for her husband. And I heard a great voice out of heaven saying, Behold, the tabernacle of God is with men, and he will dwell with them, and they shall be his people, and God himself shall be with them, and be their God. And God shall wipe away all tears from their eyes; and there shall be no more death, neither sorrow, nor crying, neither shall there be any more pain: for the former things are passed away. And he that sat upon the throne said, Behold, I make all things new. And he said unto me, Write: for these words are true and faithful. And he said unto me, It is done. I am Alpha and Omega, the beginning and the end. I will give unto him that is athirst of the fountain of the water of life freely. He that overcometh shall inherit all things; and I will be his God, and he shall be my son."

~ **Revelations 21:1-7 (KJV)**

"Today God has done a new thing, and He has made life beautiful again according to His holy and divine will."

~ DEBORAH

DAY 16

IT'S IN YOUR HANDS

Good morning!

It's a beautiful morning, the sun is shining, and the birds are chirping, and we thank God for waking us up this morning. We thank God for breathing on His people, the breath of God. This attribute is the evidence that God is with us.

He was so kind when He took your hurt and pain, up and downs and the shakiness that you endured during the high waves, the tossing and turning during the rain and the flood and gave you His peace.

Even the trials and tribulations you've endured, even as a child, He took upon Himself. Nobody knows what you've been through; nobody knows the sleepless nights you had. Just thank God that He was with you all the way. After the terrible flood, God blessed Noah and his sons with this command, "Be fruitful and increase in number and fill the earth. Multiply on the earth and increase upon it."

God will take your hurt and pain, up and downs, ebbs, and flows of life and bless it. He will turn sorrow into fruit, place the fruits in your hand and say to you, "Be fruitful and multiply."

The Holy Spirit told me to tell His people today to show some kindness to someone, and tomorrow, sow a seed of kindness and watch it multiply. You've have been through hard times in life, and its now time to bless one another as God blessed Noah and his children.

NOW PRAISE THE LORD!

"And God blessed Noah and his sons, and said unto them, Be fruitful, and multiply, and replenish the earth."

~ Genesis 9:1 (KJV)

"And you, be ye fruitful, and multiply; bring forth abundantly in the earth, and multiply therein."

~ Genesis 9:7 (KJV)

DAY 17

A NOW WORD

Good morning!

A present help in time of need! It's to the point, and there is nothing else needing to be said.

Sometimes, you have to close the door to people until God opens the door again. If God never opens that door, it's not meant for you to step into that place again.

You never want to be in a place from which God has removed you, whether it be a job, in church or just around people with whom you once communicated. These people and certain elements are stressors in your life that are continually working against the Holy Spirit. God has created miracles for those who want to be partakers of His blessing.

Your job is done! God will certainly shut the door and open new doors in front of you. Everyone can't go with you into the plain path that God is now leading you.

MOVING FORWARD

"Not as though I had already attained, either were already perfect: but I follow after, if that I may apprehend that for which also I am apprehended of Christ Jesus. Brethren, I count not myself to have apprehended: but this one thing I do, forgetting those things which are behind, and reaching forth unto those things which are before, I press toward the mark for the prize of the high calling of God in Christ Jesus."

~ **Philippians 3:12-14 (KJV)**

DAY 18

WHAT HAVE YOU BEEN CHARGED TO DO?

Good morning!

It is three a.m., and it's quiet. I feel the presence of the Holy Spirit. He is saying, "Do not worry; I am with you all the way."

I'm doing what God has charged me to do. I have an assignment from God to write this inspiring devotional for God to help His people in a time of need.

What has God charged you to do? Are you doing it? Did He give you specific instruction to construct His masterpiece for Him, and you're not doing it? Did he tell you to turn in one direction and you went the way your heart desired?

What has God charged you to do? Whatever it is, you must operate in obedience and do it, and you must not sell out. God has commanded you to make full proof of your ministry. Do not allow man to cripple you or stop you. Departure is at hand now!

STAY FOCUSED ON THE THINGS OF GOD

"Neglect not the gift that is in thee, which was given thee by prophecy, with the laying on of the hands of the presbytery. Meditate upon these things; give thyself wholly to them; that thy profiting may appear to all. Take heed unto thyself, and unto the doctrine; continue in them: for in doing this thou shalt both save thyself, and them that hear thee."

~ Timothy 4: 14-16 (KJV)

DAY 19

THE DIVINE OPPORTUNE TIME

Good morning!

Picture yourself on a highway, traveling to the place the Holy Spirit showed you. Traffic is now massive, and frustration has set in by now. Your palms are sweating, you're confused, but instead of going east, your now traveling north, or maybe you're applying for a new job, and you find yourself walking out of the place of employment because the application is too long, now you find yourself in a place called wandering.

Have you been there before? Wondering why you're working a particular job when you feel you are supposed to be doing something different? Do you feel frustrated because your destiny seems delayed for a short time?

Often, God opens doors that allow you to see the wrong turns you have taken. Times when you went backward instead of moving forward into something you've never encountered before. God is so faithful. He will teach you to see and understand how your frustration can delay you from your destiny. The Holy Spirit will show you how to see and how to deal with your frustration and what triggers it.

Even while making the wrong turn, because of your issues, you have the desire to make things right! God is so faithful to open the door of divine opportunity for you. You could have stopped and said, "I give up!" But you keep moving forward toward the things of God. He has blessed you to move into the land that flows with milk and honey, the land He has promised you. You are now with one accord with the Holy Spirit and moving in the right direction. Thank God for the divine opportunity.

STAY FOCUSED!

"Brothers and sisters, I do not consider that I have made it my own yet; but one thing I do: forgetting what lies behind and reaching forward to what lies ahead. I press on toward the goal to win the [heavenly] prize of the upward call of god in Christ Jesus. All of us who are mature [pursuring spiritual perfection] should have this attitude. And if in any respect you have a different attitude that too god will make clear to you. Only let us stay true to what we have already attained."

~ Philippians 3:13 (AMP)

DAY 20

THE WARFARE IS OVER

Good morning!

God has given you the victory, so walk-in victory. The situations that were once worrisome to your mind have been destroyed. You are no longer the talk of the town. God has fought for you; He has won the battle and given you the victory.

God says to tell My people, "Rest in the presence of God, knowing that the King of Kings, the Lord of Lords, Jehovah Jireh, your Provider, Jehovah Nissi, the Lord is our banner, He has made a way.

Your obedience has moved God to move on your behalf. There are things God has spoken to you, things invisible to others that the Holy Spirit has allowed you to see, and things incomprehensible of God you understand that others don't. You recognize promises God has placed in your spirit, intangible things only you can feel, and they shall manifest. It's happening now. God said, "Rest for I have given you victory!"

A RESTING PLACE

"The Lord is my light and my salvation; whom shall I fear? The Lord is the strength of my life; of whom shall I be afraid? When the wicked, even mine enemies and my foes, came upon me to eat up my flesh, they stumbled and fell though an host should encamp against me, my heart shall not fear: though war should rise against me, in this will I be confident. One thing have I desired of the Lord, that will I seek after; that I may dwell in the house of the Lord all the days of my life, to behold the beauty of the Lord, and to enquire in his temple For in the time of trouble he shall hide me in his pavilion: in the secret of his tabernacle shall he hide me; he shall set me up upon a rock. And now shall mine head be lifted up above mine enemies round about me: therefore will I offer in his tabernacle sacrifices of joy; I will sing, yea, I will sing praises unto the Lord."

~ Psalms 25:1-6 (KJV)

DAY 21

REALLY! TRULY! HONESTLY!

Good morning!

Another Rhema word. The utterance of Jesus.

Be real with God. Honestly- it's time to step into truth, honestly-be honest with self to please God.

The problem is a lack of trust, and this is not of God. You don't have to show yourself as being something you will never be. When God wants to bless you with the very best He will bring it to you in His time.

Your obedience is a portion of your worship. It's a move that places fire on top of fire. Your obedience places fire on top of God, it ignites God and moves Him to operate on your behalf.

There is no need to fight with yourself; God knows. What you must remember is prayer is the weapon. What God wants us to do is "pray" because prayer unto God, will make the devil tremble, and flee. Walls will fall before a saint who can and will pray.

Remember this! What God has for you is for you. God orders the steps of a good man.

IT'S REVEALED THROUGH "WORSHIP"

"Be still, and know that I am God: I will be exalted among the heathen, I will be exalted in the earth."

~ Psalms 46:10 (KJV)

"And above all things have fervent charity among yourselves: for charity shall cover the multitude of sins."

~ 1 Peter 4:8 (KJV)

"So Boaz took Ruth, and she was his wife: and when he went in unto her, the Lord gave her conception, and she bare a son."

~ Ruth 4:13 (KJV)

"And Salmon begat Booz of Rachab; and Booz begat Obed of Ruth; and Obed begat Jesse;"

~ Matthew 1:5 (KJV)

DAY 22

YOU ARE IN THE HOUSE: A PLACE OF ENLARGEMENT AND FLOURISHING

Good morning!

People of God, I've got a sweet word for all glory carriers this morning! First, you must ask yourself this question: did God show you something big, (and I mean really big) bigger than you would ever imagine?

Sometimes you wondered, "Lord, is this real? If not remove this vision from me", but as time passed by, it's still in place. It's your spiritual imagination, and this is beyond what your mind can fathom. It's what I've blessed you with to bless your children and your children's children.

God said to tell his people, "It's real." It's all God, and He placed it in your spirit. You fed your spirit as well as the vision He's given you, and this is your set time to be blessed! You've tapped into the riches of God. The unmerited favour of God has been graced upon you. There's nothing that can stop you from the blessings of God.

The spirit of God will not lead you into a place, where the favour of God will not bless you. So, birth out the vision God has placed in you and allow God to do the rest. You are blessed!

GOD HAS BLESSED YOU WITH YOUR OWN

"And he removed from thence, and digged another well; and for that they strove not: and he called the name of it Rehoboth; and he said, For now the Lord hath made room for us, and we shall be fruitful in the land. And he went up from thence to Beersheba. And the Lord appeared unto him the same night, and said, I am the God of Abraham thy father: fear not, for I am with thee, and will bless thee, and multiply thy seed for my servant Abraham's sake. And he builded an altar there, and called upon the name of the Lord, and pitched his tent there: and there Isaac's servants digged a well."

~ Genesis 26:22-25(KJV)

DAY 23

ORIOLE GOLD: A MESSENGER OF GOD
"KNOW WHO YOU ARE"

Good morning!

You are a messenger of Christ Jesus. He has positioned you where he wants you. Even though you're in the house, you must keep a renewed mindset, and you must allow the mind of christ to rest, rule, and abide in your mind.

God has fought for you, and He has positioned you exactly where He wants you to be. He wants you to know that you do not have anything to worry about. He has positioned people in the place He ordained for them to be many years ago and there is no need to worry.

Just charge it all to God's account. He brought you to it, and He has released provisions needed for you to walk into it.

YOU'RE AN OVERCOMER

"Do not fret because of those who are evil or be envious of those who do wrong; for like the grass they will soon wither, like green plants they will soon die away. Trust in the LORD and do good; dwell in the land and enjoy safe pasture."

~ Psalms 37:1-3 CHAPTER (KJV)

"Then Nebuchadnezzar said, "Praise be to the God of Shadrach, Meshach and Abednego, who has sent his angel and rescued his servants! They trusted in him and defied the king's command and were willing to give up their lives rather than serve or worship any god except their own God. Therefore I decree that the people of any nation or language who say anything against the God of Shadrach, Meshach and Abednego be cut into pieces and their houses be turned into piles of rubble, for no other god can save in this way."Then the king promoted Shadrach, Meshach and Abednego in the province of Babylon."

~ Daniel 3:28-30 (KJV)

DAY 24

A BEAUTIFUL HOUSE

Good morning! God is AWESOME!!!!

Allow God to do a mighty work inside of you to become the person God created you to be, right now.

Sometimes you won't always see God moving on your behalf. There will be times when things seem a little foggy to you.

Have you ever thought about your disobedience or the fact that you have stopped working on the house of God, just because it's what you wanted to do, or maybe you fell in the hands of the enemy?

He is a God of order. Heaven is His throne, and the earth is His footstool. Where is this house you shall build for God?

First, God wants you to know that His house is within you; it's yourself. He's looking for a place of habitation. God is looking to bless you spiritually, what are you waiting on?

Allow God to order your footsteps. You must seek God, and all His righteousness and all these things shall be added unto you.

PROMISE DELIVERED: A BEAUTIFUL HOUSE OF PRAYER

"Do not let your hearts be troubled. You believe in God]; believe also in me. My Father's house has many rooms; if that were not so, would I have told you that I am going there to prepare a place for you? And if I go and prepare a place for you, I will come back and take you to be with me that you also may be where I am. *You know the way to the place where I am going."*

~ John 14:1-4(NIV)

"And my God will meet all your needs according to the riches of his glory in Christ Jesus."

~ Philippians 4:19 (NIV)

"On coming to the house, they saw the child with his mother Mary, and they bowed down and worshiped him. Then they opened their treasures and presented him with gifts of gold, frankincense and myrrh."

~ Matthew 2:11 (NIV)

DAY 25

UNSPEAKABLE JOY

Good morning!

Yesterday the Holy Spirit said, "You're a winner!"

Today He wants you to know He's blessed you with a divine shifting and a renewed mindset, which is a new way of thinking according to the will of God.

This declaration has brought about new beginnings in your life. The promises are manifesting in the natural as well.

What a difference a day will make. The new day is another beginning and another blessing. God has blessed you beyond what your imagination could ever allow you to see. It's not because of you; it's because of God. Remember it's all God. Unspeakable joy has come! Infinite joy, life changing joy. No one can touch you like Jesus can. Every time you feel the bubbling down in your soul, you know you've been touched by the hand of God.

OPEN YOUR MOUTH AND SPEAK!

Now at this time Mary arose and hurried to the hill country, to a city of Judah (Judea) and she entered the house of Zacharias and greeted Elizabeth. When Elizabeth heard Mary's greeting, her baby leaped in her womb; and Elizabeth was filled with the Holy Spirit and empowered by Him. And she exclaimed loudly, "Blessed [worthy to be praised] are you among women and blessed is the fruit of your womb! And how has it happened to me, that the mother of my Lord would come to me? For behold, when the sound of your greeting reached my ears, the baby in my womb leaped for joy. And blessed [spiritually fortunate and favoured by God] is she who believed and confidently trusted that there would be a fulfillment of the things that were spoken to her [by the angel sent] from the Lord."

~ Luke 1:39-45 (AMP)

DAY 26

ALL YOU NEED IS JESUS

Good morning!

It's a great morning! Here's a word for my sister's in Christ Jesus.

Ladies, you don't have to settle for less. You can always look to heaven for "the more" by developing your relationship with God. You need a connection with God, and during this relationship, He will bless you beyond measure.

God will give you your own. He will provide you with your own identity, your own richly blessed soul, and your own vision. He will bring you into your own entrepreneurship, and your own outlook on your own life. If it is His will, He will even bless you with your own husband.

So if you're looking to someone or something not ordained for your life, here is a present word in a time of need.

Let go and let God so He can richly bless you. God has the framework for your life in His hands, and he wants to shower you with blessings.

Connect with Jesus and receive the blessings of the lord according to his will. He will give you rest for you weary and sore feet. God has a foot spa ready and waiting for you.

LET GO AND LET GOD

"Come to me, all you who are weary and burdened, and I will give you rest. Take my yoke upon you and learn from me, for I am gentle and humble in heart, and you will find rest for your souls. For my yoke is easy and my burden is light."

~ Matthew 11:28 - 30 (NIV)

DAY 27

THE OLIVE: IT'S TIGHT, BUT IT'S RIGHT

Good morning!

Women of God, I have a word of encouragement from God to His women of God.

The Holy Spirit has allowed a turn to take place in your life, amid your next journey. Keep in mind, if God brought you to it, He is with you while you are in it. God will never leave you; neither will He forsake you.

God wants me to tell you, "Do not resist Him. Flow with the anointing He has placed on you. He has already conditioned you for the assignment, and He's now transitioning you from lack into His greater, it's called a place of being fruitful." Trust God amid the assignment, embrace your calling, and thank God for the blessing.

FROM CRUSHING TO FLOWING IN THE SPIRIT OF GOD

"And it was about the sixth hour, and there was a darkness over all the earth until the ninth hour. And the sun was darkened, and the veil of the temple was rent in the midst. And when Jesus had cried with a loud voice, he said, Father, into thy hands I commend my spirit: and having said thus, he gave up the ghost."

~ Luke 23:44-46(KJV)

"John the Baptist appeared in the wilderness preaching a baptism of repentance for the forgiveness of sins. And all the country of Judea was going out to him, and all the people of Jerusalem; and they were being baptized by him in the Jordan River, confessing their sins."

~ Mark 1:4-5 (KJV)

DAY 28

"GREATER" COMES IN SMALL PACKAGES

Good morning!

The sun is shining, the wind is blowing, and there's a movement in the spirit that has occurred. Because of your obedience in receiving the small assignments that God has handed you, you are going to the next level with God. Never look down on humble beginnings.

Here's a word of advice to carry with you wherever you go: whatever task God hands you, there is more to it than the human eye can see, God has the more in His hands. Be patient and know that God will deliver His revelation to you in due season. It's bigger than you think!

It was Martin Luther King that said, "If I cannot do great things, I can do small things in a great way."

God hands you the small, and in His timing, He will bless you with greater. To understand the thoughts of God, and have the mind of Christ, there must be obedience. If you seek to recognize His strategic plans to prosper you and give you an expected end, obedience is first. Even if you don't quite understand, honor obedience and receive the blessings of the Lord.

THE GREATER IS IN YOU!

"For my thoughts are not your thoughts, neither are your ways my ways, saith the Lord. For as the heavens are higher than the earth, so are my ways higher than your ways, and my thoughts than your thoughts."

~ Isaiah 55:8-9 (KJV)

"But God hath revealed them unto us by his Spirit: for the Spirit searcheth all things, yea, the deep things of God."

~ 1 Corinthians 2:10 (KJV)

"You, dear children, are from God and have overcome them, because the one who is in you is greater than the one who is in the world."

~ 1 John 4:4 (NIV)

DAY 29

RELAX! REFORM! RENEW! REJUVENATE!

Good morning

It's another beautiful morning. I will bless the Lord at all times, and His praise shall continually be in my mouth.

Sometimes in life, getting caught up in other people's problems, and the issues they suffer with can cause a draining effect in your spirit. If you continue, you may neglect yourself and the opportunities God has blessed you with daily. Today is the first day of the beginning of a new season in your life.
Let me give you the 4 r's to restoring yourself to you again; you're blessed like that!

RELAX: Kick back, get a pedicure, have your nails done, go shopping, or read a book.

REFORM: Write things down that you want in your life to change and submit it to God. Decree it and declare it to have been done in Jesus' name.

RENEW: Take the time out of your busy schedule and pray for a renewed mindset.

REJUVENATE: Begin a 7-day rejuvenation detox diet. Every day for 7-days, drink a vegetarian supplement once a day, preferably in the morning while you're in morning meditation. Substitute this drink for your morning coffee; it's healthy, and you deserve to be the best you that you can be!

GO HEALTHY AND TAKE CARE OF YOU!

"The Lord is my shepherd; I shall not want. He maketh me to lie down in green pastures: he leadeth me beside the still waters."

~ **Psalms 23:1,2 (KJV)**

"Blessed is the man that walketh not in the counsel of the ungodly, nor standeth in the way of sinners, nor sitteth in the seat of the scornful. But his delight is in the law of the Lord; and in his law doth he meditates day and night. And he shall be like a tree planted by the rivers of water, that bringeth forth his fruit in his season; his leaf also shall not wither; and whatsoever he doeth shall prosper."

~ **Psalms 1:1-3 (KJV)**

DAY 30

ANOTHER MORNING, ANOTHER BLESSING!

Good morning!

It's a blessing to be in the presence of God; after all, you've been through, you need this time with God, to hear from Him more and more each day. Only God can soothe and remove all your aches and pains away, and only God can replenish the nutrients that you've lost during your struggle. It's your time to be blessed by the best. Enjoy the vacation that God has blessed you with TODAY! It's just you and God!

Here's an encouraging word for the people of God. Whatever inspiring word God blesses you with, write it down and sow the seed, which is the word of God. Water the seed by believing and meditating on the seed, and attach your faith to the seed according to the word of God and watch God give the increase by creating a miracle designed to fit you. It's never too late.

BELIEVE AND RECEIVE, IT'S NEVER TO LATE

"For his anger endureth but a moment; in his favour is life: weeping may endure for a night, but joy cometh in the morning."

~ Psalms 30:5 (KJV)

"But this is how God fulfilled what he had foretold through all the prophets, saying that his Messiah would suffer. Repent, then, and turn to God, so that your sins may be wiped out, that times of refreshing may come from the LORD,"

~ Acts 3:18-19 (KJV)

" And the Lord smelled a sweet savour; and the Lord said in his heart, I will not again curse the ground any more for man's sake; for the imagination of man's heart is evil from his youth; neither will I again smite any more everything living, as I have done. While the earth remaineth, seedtime and harvest, and cold and heat, and summer and winter, and day and night shall not cease."

~ Genesis 8:21 - 22(KJV)

DAY 31

DO NOT FRET OR WEEP

Good morning!

I have a word from God to the people of God.

When you dig one ditch, you may as well dig many ditches because the trap you set is for you and your associates attempting to destroy someone else. To you, God says, "Stop!"

I woke up with morning worshiping the Father because He has given many of His people the pass to move forward. No longer are you in the hallway praising and worshiping God, the door is open to "production." Hannah was barren, and God shut up her wound for only a season. The adversary came against her, but oh! When Hannah went up to Shiloh and worshiped, God, granted her heart's desire. She went from a barren woman to a mighty worshiper.

People of God, when worship goes up from a pure heart, devils tremble and flee, and blessings begin flowing. Your worship and your faith in God moves stumbling blocks out of your way.

PRAYER CHANGES ALL SITUATIONS

"So Hannah rose up after they had eaten in Shiloh, and after they had drunk. Now Eli the priest sat upon a seat by a post of the temple of the LORD. And she was in bitterness of soul, and prayed unto the LORD, and wept sore.And she vowed a vow, and said, O LORD of hosts, if thou wilt indeed look on the affliction of thine handmaid, and remember me, and not forget thine handmaid, but wilt give unto thine handmaid a man child, then I will give him unto the LORD all the days of his life, and there shall no razor come upon his head. And it came to pass, as she continued praying before the LORD, that Eli marked her mouth."

~ 1 Samuel 1:9-12 (KJV)

And they rose up in the morning early, and worshipped before the LORD, and returned, and came to their house to Ramah: and Elkanah knew Hannah his wife; and the LORD remembered her. Wherefore it came to pass, when the time was come about after Hannah had conceived, that she bare a son, called his name Samuel, saying, Because I have asked him of the LORD."

~ 1 Samuel 1:19-20 (KJV)

DAY 32

IT'S TRUE

Good morning!

Sometimes you can allow yourself to oppress yourself!

Even after the enemy has departed, your mind can keep you engaged in battle. God cut them off and opened the doors for you to operate in the place to which you've been called.

It's not the devil; it's your back and forth mindset. It's in a state of doubtfulness when your mindset has not accepted the divine purpose as to why God has chosen you for the leading role. Stay focused on the things of God and not your past.

You can't continue to squeeze the dew from the fleece, that came from heaven into a bowl, look at it, and set in front of you contained in one place (you see the dew).

It's time to allow the dew to fall and cover the ground. Allow the word of God to fall and saturate nations in Jesus' name. It's time to let God use you to work His miracles.

Open your mouth and spread the gospel of Jesus Christ in the places God has opened for you.

NO DOUBT its ALL GOD THE MORNING DEW

"Gideon said to God, "If you will save Israel by my hand as you have promised— look, I will place a wool fleece on the threshing floor. If there is dew only on the fleece and all the ground is dry, then I will know that you will save Israel by my hand, as you said." And that is what happened. Gideon rose early the next day; he squeezed the fleece and wrung out the dew—a bowlful of water. Then Gideon said to God, "Do not be angry with me. Let me make just one more request. Allow me one more test with the fleece, but this time make the fleece dry and let the ground be covered with dew." That night God did so. Only the fleece was dry; all the ground was covered with dew."

~ Judges 6:36-40 (KJV)

DAY 33

THE SUN IS SHINING

Good morning!

Always remember the Son (Jesus) is always shinning!

Sometimes in life, you may encounter dark days, even after you've been delivered,

Here's an encouraging word for you today. Stay with God, and stay focused on the things God is showing you. Do not place your focus on the things of which you are unsure. You don't have to try and figure things out when the Son has already paved the path for us to know and believe, "It's already done." God will smile down on you and bless you.

God wants you to know; your time has come, people of God. There is to be no more confusion. God has done it; all you have to do is stay focused, receive the shifting, and wait on God.

No longer can the enemy oppress you. It's your time to produce. Your worship has pulled down the blessings God has for you. It's in your hands.

I CAN SEE NOW

"Trust in the LORD with all your heart and lean not on your own understanding; in all your ways submit to him, and he and he will make your paths straight."

~ Proverbs 3:5-6 (NIV)

"Then they came to Jericho. As Jesus and his disciples, together with a large crowd, were leaving the city, a blind man, Bartimaeus (which means "son of Timaeus"), was sitting by the roadside begging. When he heard that it was Jesus of Nazareth, he began to shout, "Jesus, Son of David, have mercy on me!" Many rebuked him and told him to be quiet, but he shouted even more, "Son of David, have mercy on me!" Jesus stopped and said, "Call him." So they called to the blind man, "Cheer up! On your feet! He's calling you. Throwing his cloak aside, he jumped to his feet and came to Jesus. "What do you want me to do for you?" Jesus asked him. The blind man said, "Rabbi, I want to see." "Go," said Jesus, "your faith has healed you." Immediately he received his sight and followed Jesus along the road."

~ Mark 10:46-52 (NIV)

DAY 34

IT "WAS" SPIRITUAL DROUGHT

Good morning!

As I sit here observing God's beautiful creation, I'm reminded of a bird called "the woodpecker."

I began to research the bird, discovered this bird is a very aggressive character, especially when it has its intention set on pecking a hole in a tree. Can you imagine, if this tree had feelings, how it feels after being beaten up by this beautiful woodpecker?

The Holy Spirit has allowed me to see; this is how many of his children feel right now. God's people can feel beat up and abused by others, on the job, in churches, and even in their homes. Be it a spouse, children, or even so-called friends. The problem is that people mistreat other people who are diligently seeking God's face.

God has a word just for you if you're feeling less than the numerator, or your self- esteem has gone from five to zero. Read what God has for you and remember to always encourage yourself with the word God has left us to use as a weapon against the wiles of the devil.

HOLD ON TO YOUR KEYS

"To the angel of the church in Philadelphia write:These are the words of him who is holy and true, who holds the key of David. What he opens no one can shut, and what he shuts no one can open. I know your deeds. See, I have placed before you an open door that no one can shut. I know that you have little strength, yet you have kept my word and have not denied my name. I will make those who are of the synagogue of Satan, who claim to be Jews though they are not, but are liars—I will make them come and fall at your feet and acknowledge that I have loved you. Since you have kept my command to endure patiently, I will also keep you from the hour of trial that is going to come on the whole world to test the inhabitants of the earth. I am coming soon. Hold on to what you have, so that no one will take your crown. The one who is victorious I will make a pillar in the temple of my God. Never again will they leave it. I will write on them the name of my God and the name of the city of my God, the new Jerusalem, which is coming down out of heaven from my God; and I will also write on them my new name. Whoever has ears, let them hear what the Spirit says to the churches."

~ Revelation 3:7-13

"God wants you to know; your time has come, people of God. There is to be no more confusion. God has done it; all you have to do is stay focused, receive the shifting, and wait on God."

~ DEBORAH

DAY 35

A "TURN"

Good morning!

Many times, the Holy Spirit will lead you in a different direction than you had initially planned! A turn, and after you've accomplished all He has for you in that season, He will say, "It's time to turn."

In this turn, you will realize you've turned into a place that you never been before — the destination the devil was trying so hard to block. But guess what? You're in there now, it's done, and you will begin to network with people that will help you step into your destiny.

Just bless the Lord, because it may not be your time according to what the world may think, but according to the Holy Spirit, it's your turn. You are blessed and highly esteemed by God.

A PLACE OF REST

"Thou in thy mercy hast led forth the people which thou hast redeemed: thou hast guided them in thy strength unto thy holy habitation. The people shall hear and be afraid: sorrow shall take hold on the inhabitants of Palestina. Then the dukes of Edom shall be amazed; the mighty men of Moab, trembling shall take hold upon them; all the inhabitants of Canaan shall melt away. Fear and dread shall fall upon them; by the greatness of thine arm they shall be as still as a stone; till thy people pass over, O Lord, till the people pass over, which thou hast purchased. Thou shalt bring them in, and plant them in the mountain of thine inheritance, in the place, O Lord, which thou hast made for thee to dwell in, in the Sanctuary, O Lord, which thy hands have established. The Lord shall reign for ever and ever."

~ Exodus 15:13-18 (KJV)

"And they came to Elim, where were twelve wells of water, and threescore and ten palm trees: and they encamped there by the waters."

~ Exodus 15:27 (KJV)

DAY 36

LOST IS NOT AN OPTION

Good morning!

I have a mighty word for today, and when God dropped it in my spirit, it was such a blessing to me, I knew I had to share it with you. God said, "Lost is not an option." Everyone should know their purpose in life.

Knowing our purpose in life will most definitely eradicate the case of lost momentum to which we can fall a victim. It's miserable to be in a position where you are not seeing a movement of God, and you seem to be circling with no vision or direction in life, the same thing happening over and over again.

The devil loves to see people of God lost in the wilderness.

To know your purpose is to develop a closer relationship with God continually, and it's our everyday blessing.

Every day we should go higher and higher in the things of God and not in the things of the world.

It is time to regain your momentum. The only way it can be done is by the Spirit of the living God. Ask God to direct your path. It's not about you, but it's all about God.

LET GOD LEAD THE WAY

"Then he answered and spake unto me, saying, This is the word of the LORD unto Zerubbabel, saying, Not by might, nor by power, but by my spirit, saith the LORD of hosts."

~ Zechariah 4:6

DAY 37

IT'S NOT WHAT IT LOOKS LIKE

Good morning!

It's a glorious morning, and the Spirit of God is all over you. Yes, you!

God wants to use you as his vessel. I feel safe to say, at some point in life, as you are diligently seeking God for the "things of God," the adversary will attempt to attack you with the intentions of confusion. Remember, God is not the author of confusion; God is your hope for tomorrow. You must remember to stay focused on God, even amid adversity. There is no need to doubt. Keep in mind and never forget that God is your everything. He's your rock in a weary land, He's a shelter in the time of need, He's your joy, and He is your lawyer in the courtroom. He's your healer and your deliverer, and you can call on Jesus anytime. God will pick you up and place your feet on solid ground, because He is your health and strength, and He will let you know he's there. God is your everything.

Never give up hope, and don't ever think you are alone. You may not see Him, but He's always there with you. This is your inheritance.

A TEST OF FAITH "NEVER LOSE HOPE"

"Though he slay me, yet will I trust in him: but I will maintain mine own ways before him."

~ Job 13:15 (KJV)

"Canst thou draw out leviathan with an hook? or his tongue with a cord which thou lettest down?"

~ Job 41: 1 (KJV)

"Then Job answered the Lord, and said, I know that thou canst do every thing, and that no thought can be withholden from thee. Who is he that hideth counsel without knowledge? therefore have I uttered that I understood not; things too wonderful for me, which I knew not. Hear, I beseech thee, and I will speak: I will demand of thee, and declare thou unto me. I have heard of thee by the hearing of the ear: but now mine eye seeth thee. Wherefore I abhor myself, and repent in dust and ashes."

~ Job 42:1-6 (KJV)

DAY 38

SPIRITUAL AWAKENING

Good morning!

God has awakened me with a marvellous word for you!

I heard the Holy Spirit say to me, "Many of my people are awakened early in the morning, and they are unable to return to sleep." God began to speak to me and said to write these words.

"I am great," "I am," and, "I am waking you up to bless you, and for some of you, I want to give you the plan I have for your life. Some of you I'm calling, and you will not answer, some answer and do not understand. There's some I want to give the strategic plan I have for their life, and my plans are to prosper you." God said some of His people would not open their eyes, and in fact, they refuse to open their eyes.

Allow me to encourage you, upon rising early in the morning, at your wake-up call, give God the first fruit of your day and begin to talk to God, and he will answer you back. Yes, Lord!

GOD'S PLAN BRINGS DIVINE PURPOSE "A NEW THING"

"For I know the thoughts that I think toward you, saith the Lord, thoughts of peace, and not of evil, to give you an expected end."

~ Jeremiah 29:11 (KJV)

"Now Samuel did not yet know the Lord, neither was the word of the Lord yet revealed unto him. And the Lord called Samuel again the third time. And he arose and went to Eli, and said, here am I; for thou didst call me. And Eli perceived that the Lord had called the child. Therefore Eli said unto Samuel, Go, lie down: and it shall be, if he call thee, that thou shalt say, Speak, Lord; for thy servant heareth. So Samuel went and lay down in his place. And the Lord came, and stood, and called as at other times, Samuel, Samuel. Then Samuel answered, Speak; for thy servant heareth, And the Lord said to Samuel, Behold, I will do a thing in Israel, at which both the ears of every one that heareth it shall tingle."

~ 1 Samuel 3:7-11 (KJV)

DAY 39

SPEAK LIFE TODAY

Good morning!

Like always, the Holy Spirit is speaking loud!

I pray you will be blessed by the word He is giving me to bless you with. God says, speak life into your own life. It's your time, and He wants to bless you. You've been speaking life and calling things that be not as though they were in other's lives, seeing the manifestation, along with testimonies, and you understand it's not for your glory, but to God, be all the glory.

It's your time to call those things into divine alignment in your own life. Do not forget about your health, and things will line up according to God's will. Death and life are in the power of the tongue. You've been taught by the best to speak life!

This is your season to receive blessings that God has waiting for you, and I heard God say, "You see them, now call them into existence."

It's your inheritance-by faith that receives the blessings of Abraham.

IT'S YOUR TIME TO LIVE

"So I prophesied as I was commanded: and as I prophesied, there was a noise, and behold a shaking, and the bones came together, bone to his bone. And when I beheld, lo, the sinews and the flesh came up upon them, and the skin covered them above: but there was no breath in them. Then said he unto me, Prophesy unto the wind, prophesy, son of man, and say to the wind, Thus saith the Lord God; Come from the four winds, O breath, and breathe upon these slain, that they may live. So I prophesied as he commanded me, and the breath came into them, and they lived, and stood up upon their feet, an exceeding great army. Then he said unto me, Son of man, these bones are the whole house of Israel: behold, they say, Our bones are dried, and our hope is lost: we are cut off for our parts. Therefore prophesy and say unto them, Thus saith the Lord God; Behold, O my people, I will open your graves, and cause you to come up out of your graves, and bring you into the land of Israel. And ye shall know that I am the Lord, when I have opened your graves, O my people, and brought you up out of your graves, And shall put my spirit in you, and ye shall live, and I shall place you in your own land: then shall ye know that I the Lord have spoken it, and performed it, saith the Lord."

~ Ezekial 37:7-14 (KJV)

"Death and life are in the power of the tongue. You've been taught by the best to speak life!"

~ DEBORAH

DAY 40

LEAN ON JESUS AT ALL TIMES

Good morning!

It's another morning, with another blessed word with God has given me to give His people.

I heard the Holy Spirit say, "Tell My people the way to stay connected to God is through His hem." His hem is a live representation of the Holy Scriptures, and it's studying to show thyself approved by God.

If you are seeking God for whatever issue you are dealing with in your personal life, your marriage, your job, or whatever the need may be, distractions will come to annoy you and separate you from spending time with God. Cast your issues and distractions on the lord, sit at the feet of Jesus, and there you will find your healing through prayer and seeking God.

Just lay yourself at Jesus' feet, and He will open the door to your healing.

TIME WITH JESUS AND RECOGNIZE THE HIS PRESENCE

"Now it came to pass, as they went, that he entered into a certain village: and a certain woman named Martha received him into her house. And she had a sister called Mary, which also sat at Jesus' feet, and heard his word.But Martha was cumbered about much serving, and came to him, and said, Lord, dost thou not care that my sister hath left me to serve alone? bid her therefore that she help me. And Jesus answered and said unto her, Martha, Martha, thou art careful and troubled about many things: But one thing is needful: and Mary hath chosen that good part, which shall not be taken away from her."

~ Luke 10:38-42 (KJV)

DAY 41

THE NEEDFUL THING

Good morning!

It is truly a blessing to have and to keep a connection with God.

He wants His people to know Him and to feel the presence around us, not just around us but within our temple.

It's like a bubbling sensation; you can even feel it on your lips, giving you the unction to speak life into others.

Stay connected to God and allow God to use you to do His will.

MAKE YOUR HOME AT THE FEET OF JESUS

"But one thing is needful: and Mary hath chosen that good part, which shall not be taken away from her."

~ Luke 10:42 (KJV)

"He that believeth on me, as the scripture hath said, out of his belly shall flow rivers of living water."

~ John7:38 (KJV)

DAY 42

I SEE THE LORD WORKING

Good morning!

I am so glad we can be endowed with God's blessings, wisdom, knowledge, and understanding instead of stumbling in life and not understanding why we go through the things we go through!

It's a blessing for God's people to see the things God has set before them and to follow the directions He gives.

God is still giving sight to the Blind. What He did for blind Bartimaeus, He'll do for you. Just Continue to Worship God!

JESUS HEARD YOUR CRY

"But they that wait upon the LORD shall renew their strength; they shall mount up with wings as eagles; they shall run, and not be weary; and they shall walk, and not faint."

~ Isaiah 40:31(KJV)

"And Jesus stood still, and commanded him to be called. And they call the blind man, saying unto him, Be of good comfort, rise; he calleth thee. And he, casting away his garment, rose, and came to Jesus. And Jesus answered and said unto him, What wilt thou that I should do unto thee? The blind man said unto him, Lord, that I might receive my sight. And Jesus said unto him, Go thy way; thy faith hath made thee whole. And immediately he received his sight, and followed Jesus in the way."

~ Mark 10:49:52(KJV)

DAY 43

A GOOD HEART

Good morning!

A little encouragement for you today, and I pray it'll carry you to the next day and even further than that.

My encouragement for you today is, only what you do for Jesus will last.

You must make sure your heart is right with God. You must make sure you intend to please God.

If you desire to see the new life God has promised, keep your heart in good standing with Him.

WOMAN OF GOD

"The elder, To the lady chosen by God and to her children, whom I love in the truth—and not I only,

but also all who know the truth because of the truth, which lives in us and will be with us forever: Grace, mercy and peace from God the Father and from Jesus Christ, the Father's Son, will be with us in truth and love. It has given me great joy to find some of your children walking in the truth, just as the Father commanded us. And now, dear lady, I am not writing you a new command but one we have had from the beginning. I ask that we love one another. And this is love: that we walk in obedience to his commands. As you have heard from the beginning, his command is that you walk in love."

~ 2 John 1:1-6 (NIV)

"Blessed are the Pure in heart for they shall see God."

~ Matthew 5:8 (KJV)

DAY 44

PRAYER

Good morning!

People of God, it is necessary to pray every day.

If you don't pray, you should begin to incorporate prayer into your daily schedule; it should be an essential part of everyone's life.

Prayer is the key along with your faith that unlocks doors that's an essential part of our identity, discovering who we are in Christ Jesus. Pray and don't ever stop praying, allow prayer to become a large part of your life. Pray!

Reasons why you should **PRAY**:

Partnership with Jesus (your way of communication)

Revelations (you will partner with God, and he will begin to reveal His mysteries to you.

Assignment given to you by God, you are chosen to "pray.

You are a prayer warrior, anointed to pray, and you will see manifestation according to the word that has already been spoken.

YOUR "IT" HAS ARRIVED "IT'S" WHAT YOU PRAYED FOR

"I exalt you, Lord for you have lifted me up, and my enemies could not gloat over me. Lord, my God, I cried out to you for help and you healed me. Lord, you brought me from death; you kept me alive so that I did not descend into the Pit. You, his godly ones, sing to the Lord, give thanks at the mention of his holiness For his wrath is only momentary; yet his favor is for a lifetime. Weeping may lodge for the night, but shouts of joy will come in the morning. As for me I said in my prosperity "I will never be moved." By your favor, Lord, you established me as a strong mountain; Then you hid your face and I was dismayed."

~ **Psalms 30:1-6 (NIV)**

DAY 45

JESUS TAKES YOU TO THE NEXT LEVEL: LET THE HOLY GHOST LEAD YOU

Good morning!

I heard The Holy Spirit say, "Tell my people, I still hover over darkness." God still moves over the dark areas in our lives, and the places of confusion, and He still works where there is uncertainty and lack. The one thing we must understand is how important it is for us to **RECOGNIZE** the presence of God. When we recognize His presence, He will begin to shine the light on the darkness in our life.

"The light has come."

~ Romans 14:22-23(MSG)

Cultivate your relationship with God, but don't impose it on others. You're fortunate if your behaviour and your belief are coherent. If you're not sure, you will notice you are acting in ways inconsistent with what you believe. If you find on some days you are trying to impose your opinions on others, and on other days you are just trying to please them—then you know that you're out of line. If the way you live isn't consistent with what you believe, then it's wrong.

DAY 46

THE FAVOR OF GOD

Good morning!

This message is short, but it is so sweet!

God shows great favour to those that fear the Lord! Yes, He does, and He will give you the desires of your heart according to His will.

THE BIRTHING PLACE "YOUR WORSHIP"

"Wherefore it came to pass, when the time was come about after Hannah had conceived, that she bare a son, and called his name Samuel, saying, Because I have asked him of the LORD."

~ 1 Samuel 20:1 (KJV)

"And she said, Oh my lord, as thy soul liveth, my lord, I am the woman that stood by thee here, praying unto the LORD. For this child I prayed; and the LORD hath given me my petition which I asked of him: Therefore also I have lent him to the LORD; as long as he liveth he shall be lent to the LORD. And he worshipped the LORD there."

~ 1 Samuel 1:26-28 (KJV)

DAY 47

SHORT FUSES

Good morning!

We all battle with those little irritants that come to derail us from moving forward in the things of God, but the Holy Spirit wants you to know He is here for you.

The Lord will help you to stand firm, and He will give you the strength to make it through.

You must always remember, He is here for you in the midst of servitude, doing His work, and knowing His work never goes unfinished.

A GRATEFUL PRAISE

"Serve the LORD with gladness: come before His presence with singing."

~ Psalms 100:2 (KJV)

"Praise ye the LORD. Sing unto the LORD a new song, and his praise in the congregation of saints."

~ Psalms 149:1 (KJV)

"Shout for joy to the lord, all ye earth."

~ Psalms 100:1 (NIV)

"Worship the lord with gladness; come before him with joyful songs."

~ Psalms 100:2 (NIV)

"His lord said unto him, Well done, good and faithful servant; thou hast been faithful over a few things, I will make thee ruler over many things: enter thou into the joy of thy Lord."

~ Matthew 25:23 (KJV)

DAY 48

A GOOD WOMAN BUILDS HER OWN HOUSE

Good morning!

When you are creating your fulfilment in God, you will not feel the need to peep and see what others are doing in life; you will be so busy doing your own. When you mind your own business, moving in the direction, God has pathed for you.

Don't miss out on your own, paying attention to others.

WAVES OF CHANGE BRINGS WAVES OF BLESSINGS IN YOUR LIFE.

"Now there cried a certain woman of the wives of the sons of the prophets unto Elisha, saying, Thy servant my husband is dead; and thou knowest that

thy servant did fear the LORD: and the creditor is come to take unto him my two sons to be bondmen."And Elisha said unto her, What shall I do for thee? tell me, what hast thou in the house? And she said, Thine handmaid hath not anything in the house, save a pot of oil.Then he said, Go, borrow thee vessels abroad of all thy neighbours, even empty vessels; borrow not a few. And when thou art come in, thou shalt shut the door upon thee and upon thy sons, and shalt pour out into all those vessels, and thou shalt set aside that which is full. So she went from him, and shut the door upon her and upon her sons, who brought the vessels to her; and she poured out. And it came to pass, when the vessels were full, that she said unto her son, Bring me yet a vessel. And he said unto her, There is not a vessel more. And the oil stayed. Then she came and told the man of God. And he said, Go, sell the oil, and pay thy debt, and live thou and thy children of the rest."

~ 2 Kings 4:1-7 (KJV)

DAY 49

GOOD CHOICES

Good morning!

When God gives you a choice, then you must seek after the things of God in that choice and not the things of man.

Go in the direction God has given you and not in the direction man thinks best for you.

The best choices are always seen and directed by God.

So remember! "If God is giving you the choices, then you must seek after the things of God and not the things of man."

THE THINGS OF GOD

"Now faith is the substance of things hoped for, the evidence of things not seen."

~ Hebrews 11:1 (KJV)

"Then she came and told the man of God. And he said, Go, sell the oil, and pay thy debt, and live thou and thy children of the rest."

~ 2 Kings 4:7 (KJV)

"Now unto him that is able to do exceeding abundantly above all that we ask or think, according to the power that worketh in us."

~ Ephesians 3:20 (KJV)

DAY 50

ALLOW THE HOLY GHOST TO WORK IN YOU ALWAYS

Good morning!

Don't miss out on your directions and instructions, and the understanding that the Holy Spirit is fighting for you. God is blessing you with an outpouring of His wisdom and instructions.

Sometimes you can allow the waves of negativity to block your path, but don't bow down to your frustration, anger, or your emotions. When you live in that mindset, you can't see or hear what God has for you. That wave of attack is the adversary.

Just take whatever negativity you are dealing with and give it to God, because He is here to bless His people. Be silent and move in silence. Keep your focus on God and allow His spirit to unleash His uncommon favor on you like never before.

WORK ON ME LORD

"Nevertheless the foundation of God standeth sure, having this seal, The Lord knoweth them that are his. And, let every one that nameth the name of Christ depart from iniquity. But in a great house there are not only vessels of gold and of silver, but also of wood and of earth; and some to honour, and some to dishonour. If a man therefore purge himself from these, he shall be a vessel unto honour, sanctified, and meet for the master's use, and prepared unto every good work. Flee also youthful lusts: but follow righteousness, faith, charity, peace, with them that call on the Lord out of a pure heart."

~ 2 Timothy 2:19-20 (KJV)

"For I say unto you, that this that is written must yet be accomplished in me, And he was reckoned among the transgressors: for the things concerning me have an end."

~ Luke 22:37 (KJV)

"Blessed are the pure in heart: for they shall see God."

~ Matthew 5:8 (KJV)

DAY 51

WHAT'S ON YOUR MIND?

Good morning!

When God has work for you to do, know the wiles of the devil will come your way. Satan will plant negative thoughts flowing through your mind because the enemy would like to deceive you by saying you don't have the ability to what you're called to do. He will tell you that you are not equipped, or you may even hear him say, that's not God calling you.

I want to encourage you today! You are who God has called you to be! God has equipped you to do His work, and there is nothing to do but to do it. You were designed to do all God has called you to do.

JUST DO IT

"For as he thinketh in his heart, so is he: Eat and drink, saith he to thee; but his heart is not with thee."

~ Proverbs 23:7(KJV)

"Trust in the LORD with all thine heart; and lean not unto thine own understanding."

~ Philippians 4:13 (KJV)

"And blessed is she that believed: for there shall be a performance of those things which were told her from the Lord."

~ Luke 1:45(KJV)

DAY 52

THE MORE YOU GIVE, THE MORE GOD WILL GIVE TO YOU.

Good morning!

Another morning, another blessing! God is good, and He is far better to us than we are to ourselves.

I heard the spirit of God saying to me this morning to give to the least of them all. There are so many people, and organizations currently operating in their purpose of assisting those in need of food, clothing, and other resources, but are lacking funds. God sees the need, and while their struggles are real, and I'm so happy that God has made a way. He gives divine instructions with divine interventions, to God be all the glory.

Sometimes people overlook God for their divine instruction in operating businesses, especially when it's given to them by God.

Today, we thank God for all He has done to meet the needs of His people.

Continue to stay focused on God and remember to bless, always stay connected to the source; it's God.

GOD IS THE PROBLEM SOLVER

"God hates cheating in the marketplace; he loves it when business is aboveboard. A thick bankroll is no help when life falls apart, but a principled life can stand up to the worst."

~ Proverbs 11:1 (MSG)

"God's blessing makes life rich; nothing we do can improve on God."

~ Proverbs 10:22 (MSG)

"Elisha said, "Go around and ask all your neighbors for empty jars. Don't ask for just a few. Then go inside and shut the door behind you and your sons. Pour oil into all the jars, and as each is filled, put it to one side." She left him and shut the door behind her and her sons. They brought the jars to her and she kept pouring. When all the jars were full, she said to her son, "Bring me another one." But he replied, "There is not a jar left." Then the oil stopped flowing. She went and told the man of God, and he said, "Go, sell the oil and pay your debts. You and your sons can live on what is left."

~ 2 kings 3-7(NIV)

DAY 53

THE GOOD DEED

Good morning!

It's a blessing to receive a good feeling when you do good deeds for those who need a blessing. This morning I received a text message from somebody dear to my heart who asked me, "How do I obtain a copy of the book you wrote, waves of change?" God dropped it in my spirit to send him a copy free. Without a doubt, I texted him back, asking for his address and informing him I will send a copy free of charge. He then responded with much excitement, "Are you serious? I thank you so much!!!"

I know he thanked me, and he's been through a life-threatening illness, but God brought him out without a doubt. He has been made free. Sometimes there's knowledge God will impart in our spirit through books he has allowed his people to scribe.

It was a blessing to me to know I'm being used by God to bless someone God has a blessing for in the book. It's not about the sale of a book; it's about the divine impartation to lead to transformation, from not knowing to understanding God's relationship in repositioning.

YOU ARE WHO WHAT GOD SPOKE IN THE BEGINNING.

"In the beginning God created the heaven and the earth. And the earth was without form, and void; and darkness was upon the face of the deep. And the Spirit of God moved upon the face of the waters. And God said, Let there be light: and there was light."

~ Genesis 1:1-3 (KJV)

"And Moses said unto God, Who am I, that I should go unto Pharaoh, and that I should bring forth the children of Israel out of Egypt?"

~ Exodus 3:11 (KJV)

"Now Moses kept the flock of Jethro his father in law, the priest of Midian: and he led the flock to the backside of the desert, and came to the mountain of God, even to Horeb."

~ Exodus 3:1(KJV)

"Then the word of the Lord came unto me, saying, Before I formed thee in the belly I knew thee; and before thou camest forth out of the womb I

sanctified thee, and I ordained thee a prophet unto the nations."

~ Jeremiah 1:4-5

"Sometimes people overlook God for their divine instruction in operating businesses, especially when it's given to them by God."

~ DEBORAH

DAY 54

NO REASON TO PRETEND!

Good morning!

Live your dreams accordingly to the name of Jesus. Be patient and wait on God. He will shift you into your dreams, and you will begin to see manifestations.

With all your pursuits and ambitions, you must obtain wisdom, knowledge, and understanding. It's there for the asking.

You must be persistent in the blessing of studying the word of God.

Believing in your dreams no matter what comes your way, continue to believe.

Understanding that when God shifts, His timings and His purpose, He is connecting you with the Holy Spirit, where you will see the fulfilment of what God has spoken in your life.

THY WILL BE DONE

"But they that wait upon the LORD shall renew their strength; they shall mount up with wings as eagles; they shall run, and not be weary; and they shall walk, and not faint."

~ Isaiah 40:31 (KJV)

"Blessed is she who has believed that the Lord would fulfill his promises to her!"

~ Luke 1:45 (NIV)

"Jesus turned and saw her."Take heart, daughter," he said, "your faith has healed you." And the woman was healed at that moment."

~ Matthew 9:22 (NIV)

DAY 55

A COOL BREEZE

Good morning!

Sometimes when you become weary in life, and it may appear as though you're on your last leg, on the edge of fainting, but because God is so faithful to his people, He will bless you with a way of escape.

God will send a cool breeze, the breath of life on His people. He does this just to let you know, "I am with you" "I will never leave you, nor will I forsake you."

Often we think He hasn't answered what we have prayed for, and that's when faith should step in. Before your doubt takes over, only you can activate your faith in God by worshiping the true and living God.

It's not about the promise; it's about your worship. Your praise and worship unto the true and living God will cause shifting in your atmosphere from a stressing place to a blessing place.

AN ANSWERED PRAYER

"And let us not be weary in well doing: for in due season we shall reap, if we faint not."

~ Galatians 6:9 (KJV)

"God is a Spirit: and they that worship him must worship him in spirit and in truth."

~ John 4:24 (KJV)

DAY 56

HAPPY BIRTHDAY!!!

Good morning!

As I was waiting on the Holy Spirit to deliver a word to me today, He placed a Happy Birthday in my heart. So, I'd like to take the time out to tell everyone whose birthday is in September, **"HAPPY BIRTHDAY AND MAY THE GOOD LORD BLESS YOU REAL GOOD."**

This is my birthday month, and I want to share a sneak preview of what's to come.

I want to tell you something significant. God does not allow you to write without purpose; you never know what God has in store for His people until you humble yourself and allow God to use you according to His will.

God speaks to those He has anointed to write and those He has anointed to hear and what He's saying for such a time as this.

God is Good, He is great, and He is worthy to be worshiped. Let us be thirsty for the things of God, like never before.

September is my birthday month, and I requested a sneak preview of what's to come.

God Bless you and yours, and I pray this 56day inspirational devotional is a blessing in your life

GOD'S BLESSINGS

"The Lord bless thee, and keep thee: The Lord make his face shine upon thee, and be gracious unto thee: The Lord lift up his countenance upon thee, and give thee peace. And they shall put my name upon the children of Israel, and I will bless them."

~ Numbers 6:24-26 (KJV)

"For all the promises of God in him are yea, and in him Amen, unto the glory of God by us. Now he which established us with you in Christ, and hath anointed us, is God; Who hath also sealed us,and given the earnest of the Spirit in our hearts."

~ 1 Corinthians 1:20-22 (KJV)

MY GIFT TO YOU

PRAYER

I pray this book has spiritually blessed your soul, and I pray that the blessing of the Lord overtakes you in the natural as well.

I pray god gives you strength to endure the race He has set before you.

I pray you stay focused on the things of God. I pray a tsunami of God's promises over-takes you, that and you will have no other choice but to call on your partners to assist you in the partaking of kingdom work/kingdom building, and every work God has destined you to do.

In Jesus name, we thank you for your victory, and we know all victory belongs to you.

God is good, and he is worthy to be worshiped!

CPSIA information can be obtained
at www.ICGtesting.com
Printed in the USA
LVHW021042041119
636249LV00002B/555